Live In Wonder

A Journal of Quests, Quotes, & Questions to Jumpstart Your Journey

ERIC SAPERSTON

with MIRABELLA LOVE

PETER PAUPER PRESS, INC.
WHITE PLAINS, NEW YORK

A special thanks goes out to all of you who, along this
magical journey, gave me a couch to sleep on, a word of
encouragement, or a few bucks for gas and dog food.
You folks know who you are and how much you mean to me.
With love and gratitude, I thank you all.

This book is dedicated to my mom.

First published by Live In Wonder Press in 2009.

This edition first published by Peter Pauper Press in 2014,
copyright © 2014 by Eric Saperston, liveinwonder.com.

Cover illustration copyright © donatas 1205.
Used under license from Shutterstock.com

Peter Pauper Press, Inc.
202 Mamaroneck Avenue
White Plains, NY 10601
ISBN 978-1-4413-1419-2
Printed in China
7 6 5 4 3 2

Visit us at www.peterpauper.com

You are the same today as you'll be in five years
except for two things,
the books you read and the people you meet.

Charlie "Tremendous" Jones

THE QUEST

R emember when Alice was lost in Wonderland? She serendipitously stumbled upon the Cheshire Cat and asked which way she should go. With a wry grin, the Cheshire Cat responded by telling her that it depended on where she wanted to get to. To which Alice replied that she didn't much care so long as she got somewhere. Grinning from ear to ear, the insightful cat dropped some clever wisdom and told her that if she wasn't sure where she was going, then any road would take her there.

This book is not just about taking any road. This book is about taking *your* road, your adventure, your journey, your quest.

Consider this bundle of pages to be your traveling companion to anyplace worthwhile. Its sole purpose is to be a guide and a tool for the discovery of your highest truth and your deepest gifts, and how to use them both to be of service to the world.

Your journey begins with "The Quest," the basic premise of which is this: the quickest and surest way to become anything you want in life is to make a fearless assessment of where you are, imagine where you want to be, and learn from those who have already succeeded on a path you admire.

Maybe you've always wanted to make a movie, build a boat, or live in India. Maybe you want to be a rock star, start a non-profit, or write a children's book. Or maybe you're just curious about the meaning of life. Whatever you desire, whatever it is that's calling you from the depths of your soul, now is the time to trust that inner voice and follow the call to adventure.

Spend time getting to know yourself. Ask yourself hard questions. To go anywhere, you first need to understand where you've come from and what you're taking with you on your new adventure. More importantly, never be afraid to ask for help. Other people are the most incredible resource available to you. My personal experience has taught me that anything you want to learn or be in this world is possible because everything you need to know is only a cup of coffee and an inspired conversation away. There's an old Chinese proverb that says it even more succinctly: "To know the road ahead, ask those coming back."

An inquisitive mind and a humble heart are all the permission and credentials you'll need to call on the powerful and passionate people whom you respect and admire. Invite them out for a cup of coffee so you can learn from their experiences. If the person you admire is unavailable to you, read their writings, learn about their journey, or visit their website. Discover the common traits, motivations, and distinguishing characteristics that have given them the strength, courage, and conviction to successfully live the lives they love.

So contemplate this: whom do you respect and admire in your life? Who is doing what it is you'd like to be doing? Whose life and lifestyle would you most like to emulate? Who's transforming the world in ways you'd like to as well? Who inspires you? Look around your world. It might be a favorite aunt or uncle, rabbi, priest, poet, politician, schoolteacher, musician, truck driver, judge, astronaut, comedian, actor, doctor, soldier, or scientist.

There is no shame in asking others for help. One of my first interviews was with the jolly and charismatic Donald Keough (a former Fortune 500 CEO), arguably one of the most successful business leaders in the world. When I asked him what separated the doers from the dreamers, his answer changed my life forever. He said, "What separates those who achieve from those who do not is in direct proportion to one's ability to ask others for help." Here I had spent my whole life believing in the phrases: "Fake it until you make it," "Never let them see you sweat," and "Only raise your hand when you are sure." Meanwhile, one of the most powerful executives on the planet was telling me: "Being vulnerable isn't a sign of weakness; it's a sign of strength. Being able to say, 'Hey, I don't know. I need your help,' is a sign of wisdom."

It might seem like an oxymoron, but in truth the quickest way to have someone respect your knowledge is to admit what you don't know. You can ask for help and be a fool for five minutes, or not ask and be a fool forever.

Wherever your curiosity and heart's longing leads you, begin right now. Your quest might take you to the famous or the not so famous, to introverts or extroverts, radicals or conservatives. Some of you will be called, like I was, to meet and interview heads of state, CEOs, presidents, poets, authors, and artists. On the other hand, a journey across the street to talk to a neighbor over a cup of coffee is equally as noble. May you use the lessons you learn to build a supportive community through spirited dialogue, as well as to gain access to the many tools you'll need to create, design, and manifest an inspired life that you love.

Your journey may take you across the street or to the Serengeti, to Vancouver or the Vatican, to Beijing or Baghdad, to New Delhi or to a deli in New York City. Wherever you go, gather as many tools, aha moments, and epiphanies as you can carry in your travel satchel. When the road is long and home is far, the words of those seasoned travelers you've met along the way will keep you going on a bad day. When you find yourself doubting your ability or second-guessing your path, the remembrance of those to whom you've reached out and their messages of encouragement will inspire you to make the impossible possible.

Remember, whatever you need, whatever you desire, whatever problem you want to solve, the answers are only a question and an inspiring conversation away.

Most of all on your journey, be patient and believe in yourself. You will meet the people you're supposed to meet, read the books you are supposed to read, and experience what you are meant to experience. So enjoy the ride and learn as much as you can along the way. No one who embarks down a path they've never taken before could possibly be aware of all the challenges, pitfalls, and wrong turns that lie ahead. That's OK. All you have to do is ask people more knowledgeable than you how to get to where you want to go. Then, have the willingness and resolve to listen and to act on what you learn.

Also, while on this quest, consider that you are the writer, director, producer, and star of your own feature film. What you think, what you say, what you believe, and how you behave determine the quality and trajectory of your life's journey. In every moment, consciously or unconsciously, you are writing your own personal story's narrative. And just like in the movies, if you were writing a screenplay about a particular hero and his or her adventure, you would need to write a host of supporting characters to help in the telling of that story. In Hollywood, everyone understands that supporting characters have but one critically important function: to reveal something about our hero that we may or may not already know about them. Consider everyone along your journey to be a wise teacher intentionally placed along your path to teach you something about yourself.

So study everything. Be curious. If someone challenges your beliefs and questions your intentions, thank them. Consider for a moment that what they are saying might actually be true and for your highest good. No matter what is said, smile and be gracious. Then, later, when you are alone, test out what was said against your own inner knowledge. If what they said was helpful, then take it. If not, then don't. It's your journey, so trust your instincts.

As you travel in the direction of your dreams, keep in mind that adventures come in all shapes and sizes. Your journey might take you on a local, state, or national quest. Your sojourn might even have you go global. Or perhaps you'll discover that your most significant and rewarding adventure happens when you meet another halfway.

One last, useful insight worth sharing: Regardless of the size, scope, and complexity of one's request, the universe always seems to answer in kind. Meaning, whatever it is you are asking for, the universe will match it. So if you ask small, you'll get small. If you ask big, you'll get big.

So cowboy up and use your lasso to wrangle the highest star possible. Then hold on because you're in for the brightest and shiniest ride of your life.

Life is a journey. Live in wonder.

THE QUOTES & THE QUESTIONS

Before embarking on any worthwhile adventure,
it may be wise to take a moment to pause and consider
a few roadworthy points from those travelers who
have gone before you, and what they have to say
about the road ahead.

Remember: If you don't know where you are going,
then any road will take you there.

May the following quotes serve as a useful compass
to help guide and lift your spirits during both
peaceful and turbulent times, as they did for me.
Each insight is followed by a related question--
many of which I used in my interviews--meant as a
catalyst for consideration and discussion.

Stuff your eyes with wonder ... live as if you'd drop dead in ten seconds. See the world. It's more fantastic than any dream made or paid for in factories.

Ray Bradbury

When have you experienced wonder in your life?

Perhaps this very instant is your time ... your own, your
peculiar, your promised and presaged moment, out of all
moments forever.

Louise Bogan

If you could dedicate your life to the one thing you're
most passionate about, what would it be?

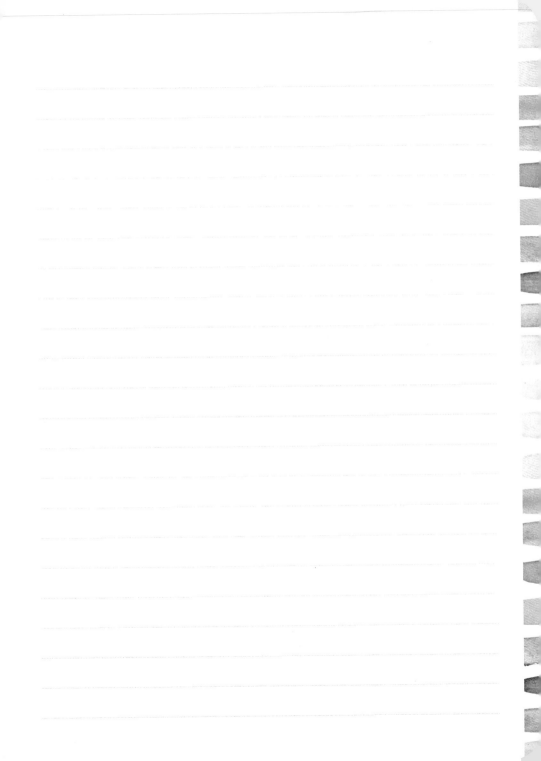

It must happen to us all. ... We pack up what we've learned so far and leave the familiar behind. No fun, that shearing separation, but somewhere within, we must dimly know that saying goodbye to safety brings the only security we'll ever know.

Richard Bach

Everyone is on a journey.
What do you need to leave behind to begin yours?

Consider what you most want in life.
What single step can you take toward it?

When in doubt, make a complete fool of yourself. There is a
microscopically thin line between being brilliantly creative
and acting like the most gigantic idiot on earth.
So what the hell, leap.

                                        Cynthia Heimel

If you knew you couldn't fail, what would you leap for?

Your time is limited, so don't waste it living someone else's life. Don't be trapped by dogma--which is living with the results of other people's thinking. Don't let the noise of others' opinions drown out your own inner voice. And most important, have the courage to follow your heart and intuition. They somehow already know what you truly want to become. Everything else is secondary.

Steve Jobs

Shine a light on the fears and insecurities that hold you back. What do they look like?

Alice laughed. "There's no use trying," she said: "one *can't* believe impossible things."
"I daresay you haven't had much practice," said the Queen.
"When I was your age, I always did it for half-an-hour a day. Why, sometimes I've believed as many as six impossible things before breakfast."

Lewis Carroll

What impossible thing would you like to make possible?

You can have anything you want--if you want it badly enough.
You can be anything you want to be, have anything you desire,
accomplish anything you set out to accomplish--if you will hold
to that desire with singleness of purpose; if you will understand
and *believe* in your own powers to accomplish.

Robert Collier

What do you see as your life's calling?

Every great discovery I ever made, I gambled that the truth was there, and then I acted on it in faith until I could prove its existence.

Arthur H. Compton

What is your most ingenious idea?

When we are upset, it's easy to blame others. However, the true cause of our feelings is within us. For example, imagine yourself as a glass of water. Now, imagine past negative experiences as sediment at the bottom of your glass. Next, think of others as spoons. When one stirs, the sediment clouds your water. It may appear that the spoon caused the water to cloud--but if there were no sediment, the water would remain clear no matter what. The key, then, is to identify our own sediment and actively work to remove it.

Josei Toda

What are you afraid to let others know about you?

Today you are You,
that is truer than true.
There is no one alive
who is Youer than You.

Dr. Seuss

What makes you **you**?

Have the courage to say no. Have the courage to face the truth.
Do the right thing because it is right. These are the magic keys
to living your life with integrity.

W. Clement Stone

When is it hardest for you to say "no"?

When someone loves you, the way they say your name is different.
You know that your name is safe in their mouth.

Jess C. Scott

What's the greatest lesson you've learned about love?

Quality questions create a quality life. Successful people ask better questions and, as a result, they get better answers.

Anthony Robbins

Identify three people you admire. What would you ask each one?

Often people attempt to live their lives backwards: they try to have more things, or more money, in order to do more of what they want so they will be happier. The way it actually works is the reverse. You must first be who you really are, then do what you need to do, in order to have what you want.

Margaret Young

What do you need to do to show who you really are?

The real challenge is not to survive. Hell, anyone can do that.
It's to survive as yourself, undiminished.

Elia Kazan

Which of your scars carries the most significance, and why?

This is the true joy in life, the being used for a purpose recognized by yourself as a mighty one; the being thoroughly worn out before you are thrown on the scrap heap; the being a force of nature instead of a feverish selfish little clod of ailments and grievances complaining that the world will not devote itself to making you happy.

George Bernard Shaw

What work brings you the greatest joy?

Heroes--in myth, literature, and real life--take journeys,
confront dragons ... and discover the treasure of their true
selves. Although they may feel very alone during the quest,
at its end their reward is a sense of community: with themselves,
with other people, and with the earth.

Carol Pearson

What was the greatest obstacle you've overcome?

Don't let yesterday use up too much of today.

Will Rogers

Any regrets? How do they slow you down?

Finish every day and be done with it. ... You have done what you could; some blunders and absurdities no doubt crept in; forget them as soon as you can. Tomorrow is a new day; you shall begin it well and serenely, and with too high a spirit to be cumbered with your old nonsense.

Ralph Waldo Emerson

How do you put past mistakes behind you?

The best way out is always through.

Robert Frost

When has perseverance served you?

What I point out to people is that it's silly to be afraid that you're not going to get what you want if you ask. Because you are already not getting what you want. They always laugh about that because they realize it's so true. Without asking you already have failed, you already have nothing. What are you afraid of? You're afraid of getting what you already have! It's ridiculous!

Marcia Martin

When was the last time you asked someone for help or advice, and what did you ask for?

If you would not be forgotten as soon as you are dead and rotten,
either write things worth reading, or do things worth writing.

Ben Franklin

What would you like to be remembered for?

Take wrong turns. Talk to strangers. Open unmarked doors. ...
There are so many adventures that you miss because you're waiting
to think of a plan. To find them, look for tiny interesting choices.

Randall Munroe

When has serendipity made a significant difference in your life?

Who are we, who is each one of us, if not a combinatoria of
experiences, information, books we have read, things imagined?

Italo Calvino

What experiences, information, or books have most influenced you?

Life is an adventure of passion, risk, danger, laughter, beauty, love, a burning curiosity to go with the action to see what it is all about, to search for a pattern of meaning, to burn one's bridges because you're never going to go back anyway, and to live to the end.

Saul D. Alinsky

What lights you up and keeps you going?

And then the day came when the risk to remain closed in a bud became more painful than the risk it took to blossom.

Elizabeth Appell

How do you know when you're ready for change?

It is a funny thing about life, if you refuse to accept anything but the best you very often get it.

W. Somerset Maugham

When have high expectations served you well?

Don't go around saying the world owes you a living; the world owes you nothing. It was here first.

Mark Twain

How can you serve the world and yourself?

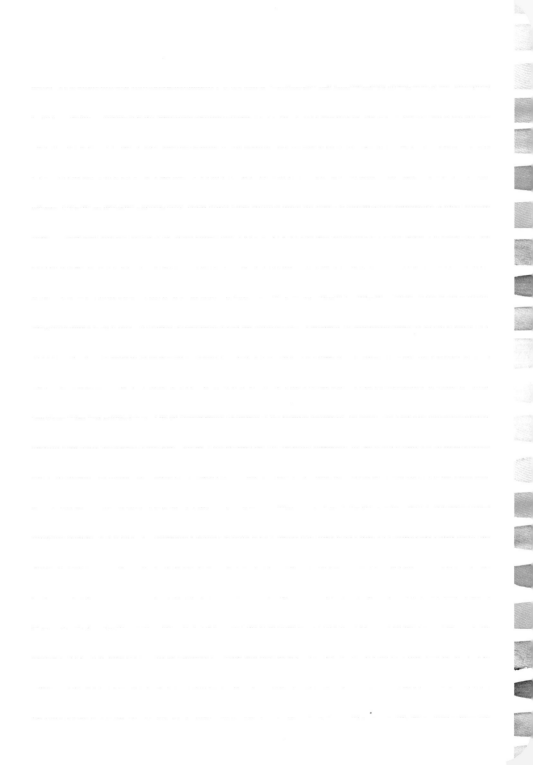

We all want to be a force for positive change. Yet, until we actually make the choice for care over indifference, faith over control, humility over ego, and uncertainty over certainty, we will be less than effective. Becoming a true evolutionary--one who is able to midwife the unmanifest potentials of life into the manifest world--requires great character, commitment, and courage.

Katherine Woodward Thomas

In your life, where are you a force for positive change?

If a child is to keep his inborn sense of wonder ... he needs the companionship of at least one adult who can share it, rediscovering with him the joy, excitement, and mystery of the world we live in.

Rachel Carson

Who has helped you to cultivate your sense of wonder?

> I can choose either to be a victim of the world or an adventurer
> in search of treasure. It's all a question of how I view my life.
>
> Paulo Coelho

How do you view your life?

The reason most people never reach their goals is that they don't define them, or ever seriously consider them as believable or achievable. Winners can tell you where they are going, what they plan to do along the way, and who will be sharing the adventure with them.

Denis Waitley

What are your top three goals, and how are you going to achieve them?

There are plenty of difficult obstacles in your path.
Don't allow yourself to become one of them.

Ralph Marston

How do you hold yourself back?

The most visible creators are those artists whose medium is life itself. The ones who express the inexpressible without brush, hammer, clay, or guitar. They neither paint nor sculpt. Their medium is being. Whatever their presence touches has increased life. They see and don't have to draw. They are the artists of being alive.

Donna J. Stone

What aspects of your life feel like a work of art?

The meaning I picked, the one that changed my life:
overcome fear, behold wonder.

Richard Bach

What are you struggling with?

The art and science of asking questions is the source of all knowledge.

Thomas Berger

You will meet many wizards on your journey. What five burning questions will you have for them?

A good laugh makes any interview, or any conversation,
so much better.

Barbara Walters

What makes you laugh?

When you plant lettuce, if it does not grow well, you don't blame
the lettuce. You look into the reasons it is not doing well.
It may need fertilizer, or more water, or less sun. You never
blame the lettuce. Yet if we have problems with our friends or our
family, we blame the other person. But if we know how to take care
of them, they will grow well, like lettuce. Blaming has no positive
effect at all, nor does trying to persuade using reason and argu-
ments. That is my experience. No blame, no reasoning, no argument,
just understanding.

Thich Nhat Hanh

What do you notice about the way you argue?

One's destination is never a place but rather a new way of looking at things.

Henry Miller

What's one new perspective you've gained in the last year?

Don't ask yourself what the world needs. Ask yourself what makes you come alive and then go do that. Because what the world needs is people who have come alive.

Howard Thurman

What makes you come alive?

Trust is the gift we give to the universe before we know what gifts it has for us in return.

Mirabella Love

What do you trust?

No pessimist ever discovered the secret of the stars, or sailed to an uncharted land, or opened a new doorway for the human spirit.

Hellen Keller

How do you create a vision so big that others will want to be a part of it?

It seems as if one never could get to the end of all the delightful things there are to know, and to observe, and to speculate about in the world. ... I still find each day too short for all the thoughts I want to think, all the walks I want to take, all the books I want to read, and all the friends I want to see.

John Burroughs

What have you started and not finished?

Life is to be lived. If you have to support yourself, you had bloody well better find some way that is going to be interesting. And you don't do that by sitting around wondering about yourself.

Katharine Hepburn

What are three vocations that interest you?

We shall not cease from exploration
And the end of all our exploring
Will be to arrive where we started
And to know the place for the first time.

T. S. Eliot

What lesson has taken you the longest to learn?

I don't believe in pessimism. If something doesn't come up the way you want, forge ahead. If you think it's going to rain, it will.

Clint Eastwood

What do you do when all else fails?

If a genie were to grant you three wishes,
what would you ask for, and why?

Regret for the things we did can be tempered by time; it is regret for the things we did not do that is inconsolable.

Sydney J. Harris

What is on your bucket list?
And when will you get started on it?

Recognize that no one is responsible for your life but you.
That you're creating your current and future reality thought
by thought. And what you give your attention to only gets bigger
and manifests itself in the world. So try to live a life focusing
on what's good and what you're grateful for, in order to have more
goodness. ... What I know for sure: you keep asking the right
questions of yourself, and the universe will unfold in ways
you never imagined.

Oprah Winfrey

What are ten things you are grateful for?

I'm not funny. What I am is brave.

Lucille Ball

What takes the most courage for you to do?

Many years ago Oprah Winfrey was interviewed about her life and asked whether she had known that she would become one of the most powerful women in the world. She explained to the reporter that when she was a little girl, someone asked her what she wanted to do with her life. She answered by saying that she didn't know. She just liked talking to people. The person quickly retorted, "Well, you can't make a living doing that."

Wayne Dyer

What could you achieve in life if you decided to become totally and blissfully impervious to unconstructive criticism and rejection?

He who is afraid of asking is ashamed of learning.

Danish proverb

What questions are you most afraid to ask?

There is a vitality, a life force, an energy, a quickening that is translated through you into action, and because there is only one of you in all of time, this expression is unique. And if you block it, it will never exist through any other medium and it will be lost. The world will not have it. It is not your business to determine how good it is nor how it compares with other expressions. It is your business to keep it yours clearly and directly, to keep the channel open.

Martha Graham

Where in your life do you let yourself be fully self-expressed?

Your journey has molded you for the greater good, and it was exactly what it needed to be. Don't think that you've lost time. There is no short-cutting to life. It took each and every situation you have encountered to bring you to the now. And now is right on time.

Asha Tyson

What huge "mistakes" have you made, and how have they served you?

Faith is taking the first step even when you don't see the
whole staircase.

Martin Luther King, Jr.

What leap of faith have you taken in your life,
and how did it play out?

This may sound too simple, but is great in consequence. Until one is committed, there is hesitancy, the chance to draw back, always ineffectiveness. Concerning all acts of initiative (and creation), there is one elementary truth, the ignorance of which kills countless ideas and splendid plans: that the moment one definitely commits oneself, then providence moves too. All sorts of things occur to help one that would never otherwise have occurred. A whole stream of events issues from the decision, raising in one's favour all manner of unforeseen incidents and meetings and material assistance, which no man could have dreamed would come his way.

William H. Murray

When was the last time you made an unwavering commitment to set your dreams in motion?

Twenty years from now you will be more disappointed by the things that you didn't do than by the ones you did do. So throw off the bowlines. Sail away from safe harbor. Catch the trade winds in your sails. Explore. Dream. Discover.

H. Jackson Brown, Jr.

What risks are you glad to have taken, and why?

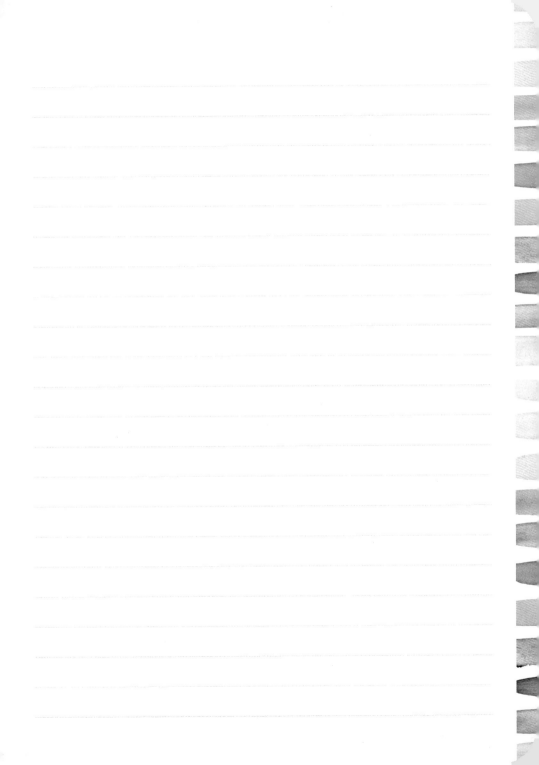

The important thing is this: to be able at any moment to sacrifice what we are for what we could become.

Charles Du Bos

Who is your hero, and why?

Don't listen to those who say, "It's not done that way." Maybe it's not, but maybe you'll do it anyway. Don't listen to those who say, "You're taking too big a chance." Michelangelo would have painted the Sistine floor, and it would surely be rubbed out by today.

Neil Simon

When have you shot for the moon and done it your way? Would you do it again?

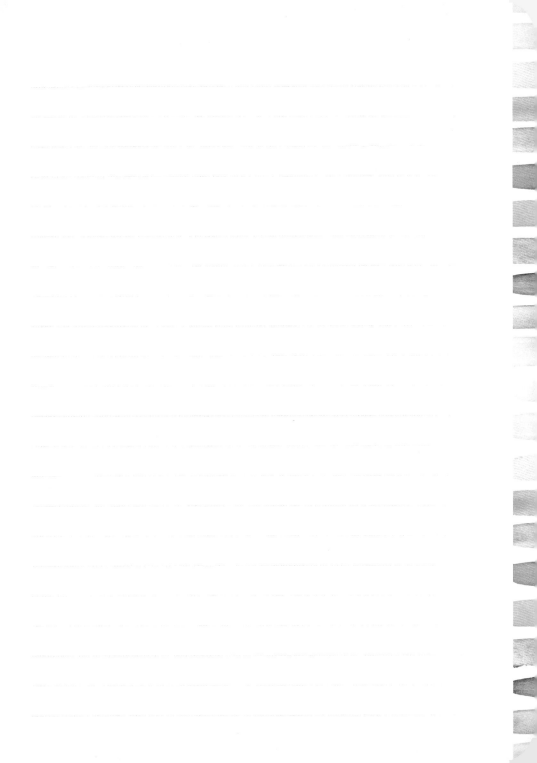

First, say to yourself who you wish to be; and then, do what you have to do.

Epictetus

Who do you wish to be? What do you have to do?

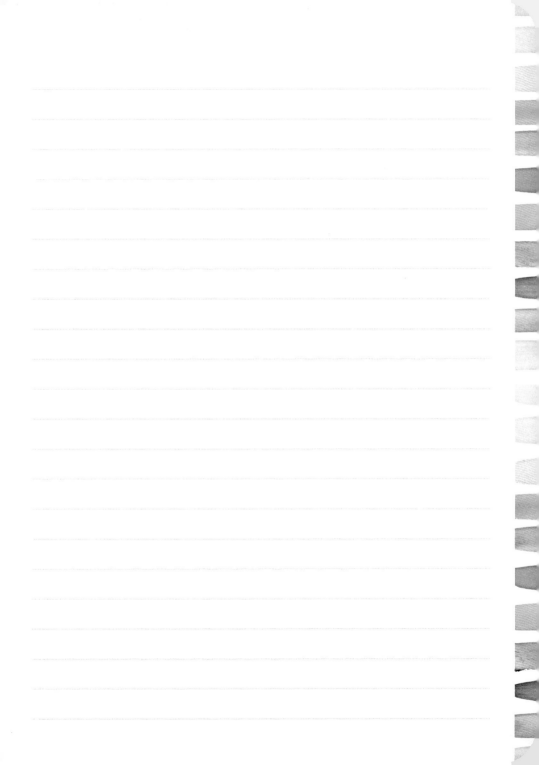

You don't get to choose how you're going to die. Or when.
But you can decide how you're going to live. Now.

Joan Baez

What's unfinished in your life, and why?

Unless you are willing to walk out into the unknown, the chances of making a profound difference in your life are pretty slim.

Tom Peters

When is a risk worth taking? What risk can you take?

Young. Old. Just words.

George Burns

What lasts forever?

What's the greatest life lesson you've learned?

Have patience with everything unresolved in your heart and try
to love the questions themselves as if they were locked rooms or
books written in a very foreign language. Don't search for the
answers, which could not be given to you now, because you would
not be able to live them. And the point is, to live everything.
Live the questions now. Perhaps then, someday far in the future,
you will gradually, without even noticing it, live your way into
the answer.

Rainer Maria Rilke

What questions do you struggle with,
and how can they best be lived?

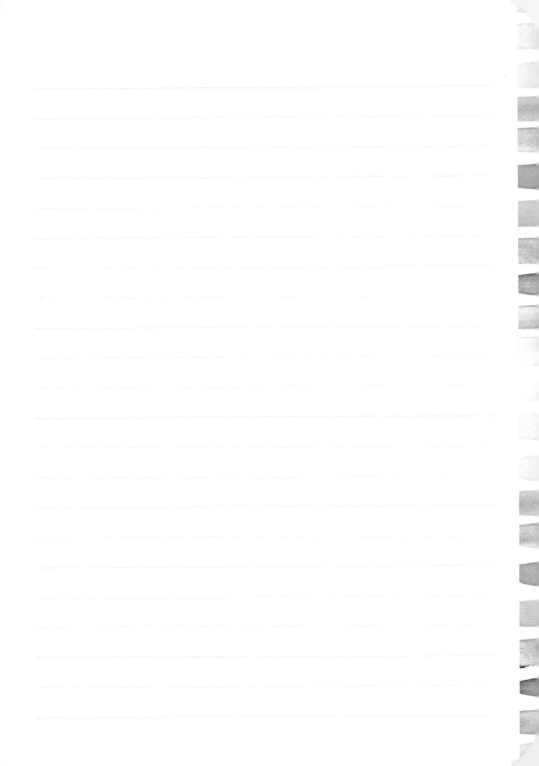

There is in you something that waits and listens for the sound of
the genuine in yourself. Nobody like you has ever been born and
no one like you will ever be born again--you are the only one. ...
So the burden of what I have to say to you is, "What is your name--
who are you--and can you find a way to hear the sound of the
genuine in yourself?"

Howard Thurman

Do you know who you genuinely are?

Forgiveness does not change the past, but it does enlarge
the future.

Paul Boese

Who in your life still needs to be forgiven?
How do you open yourself to forgiving them?

Have your adventures, make your mistakes, and choose your
friends poorly--all these make for great stories.

Chuck Palahniuk

What is your greatest story?

The important thing is not to stop questioning. Curiosity has its own reason for existence. One cannot help but be in awe when he contemplates the mysteries of eternity, of life, of the marvelous structure of reality. It is enough if one tries merely to comprehend a little of this mystery each day. Never lose a holy curiosity.

Albert Einstein

What's the purpose of life?

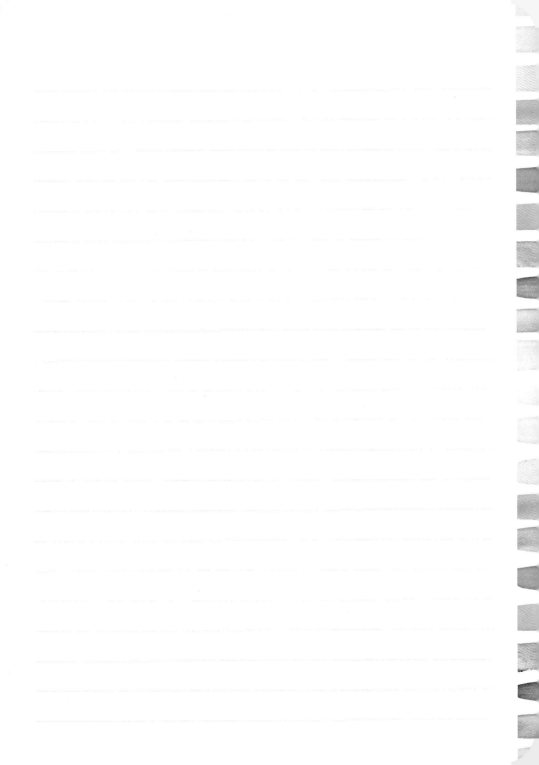

Life isn't about finding yourself. Life is about
creating yourself.

George Bernard Shaw

If you are a work in progress,
how do you continually create your life?

Security is mostly a superstition. It does not exist in nature,
nor do the children of men as a whole experience it. Avoiding
danger is no safer in the long run than outright exposure.
Life is either a daring adventure, or nothing.

Helen Keller

What adventures have you dared to take?
Were they worth it?

To be nobody-but-yourself--in a world which is doing its best, night and day, to make you everybody else--means to fight the hardest battle which any human being can fight; and never stop fighting.

e. e. cummings

How do you define yourself?

Make no comments, complaints, criticisms, appraisals, avowals, sayings, shooting stars of thought, just *flow, flow* ... shut up, live, travel, adventure, bless, and don't be sorry.

Jack Kerouac

Where to next?

The big question is whether you are going to be able to say a
hearty yes to your adventure.

Joseph Campbell

What can you do **right now** to say yes to your adventure?

ABOUT THE AUTHORS

After college, **Eric Saperston** bought a 1971 Volkswagen bus, took his golden retriever, Jack, and set out to follow the Grateful Dead and work a ski season in Aspen. While on the road he called up some of the most powerful people in the world and asked them out for a cup of coffee.

The reason: to find out the values they lived by, the struggles they endured, and what advice and counsel they would give to others to better prepare themselves for the road ahead. The result: a development deal with Walt Disney Studios, an award-winning film, *The Journey*, a speaking tour, an inspirational book, and this journal you have in your hands.

Eric Saperston is now a renowned speaker, author, and film director. He lives in a *Swiss Family Robinson*-style tree house on a 13-acre organic farm in Maui, Hawaii. He travels the globe inspiring the world to Live In Wonder.

Live In Wonder

Mirabella Love, gypsy muse. A non-linear career and life experiences have taken Mirabella from her Chicago roots and small town Indiana values to living and studying in the Middle East, building a think tank in Dallas for Cap Gemini Ernst & Young, founding Urban Pilates in San Francisco, being a fly on the wall at the innovative global design firm IDEO, editing and publishing the original *Live In Wonder* book, and incubating a platform for spiritual evolution through her collective, I Am That You Are Free. When she's not somewhere on a desert highway, her heart draws her to the Gulf Coast.

For more information, visit www.LiveInWonder.com.

PETER PAUPER PRESS
Fine Books and Gifts Since 1928

OUR COMPANY

In 1928, at the age of twenty-two, Peter Beilenson began printing books on a small press in the basement of his parents' home in Larchmont, New York. Peter—and later, his wife, Edna—sought to create fine books that sold at "prices even a pauper could afford."

Today, still family owned and operated, Peter Pauper Press continues to honor our founders' legacy—and our customers' expectations—of beauty, quality, and value.